POETIC EXPRESSIONS OF SCRIPTURE

Book by Book Poems Providing a Road Map to
New Testament Scripture

S.R. LeBrew

Copyright © 2025 S. R. LeBrew

All rights reserved.

No part of this publication may be reproduced, distributed, or transmitted in any form or by any means, including photocopying, recording, or other electronic or mechanical methods, without the prior written permission of the publisher, except in the case of brief quotations embodied in reviews and certain other non-commercial uses permitted by copyright law.

Table of Contents

Preface 1

Acknowledgments 6

The Gospels: Matthew Book 1 7

The King Has Come 7

The Gospels: Mark Book 2 10

The Passion of Christ 10

The Gospels: Luke: Book 3 13

The Compassionate Savior 13

The Gospels: John Book 4 15

The Light of The World 15

History of the early church: Acts Book 5 18

Acts of the Apostles- Anointed with Power! 18

General Epistles: Wisdom & Endurance Romans Book 6 20

By Faith, not by Works! 20

Pauline Epistles: Letter of Faith and Encouragement 1st Corinthians Book 7 22

Living as The Body of Christ 22

Pauline Epistles: Letter of Faith and Encouragement 2nd Corinthians Book 8 24

From Trials to Triumph 24

Pauline Epistles: Letter of Faith and Encouragement Galatians Book 9 26

Set Free in Christ Jesus! 26

Pauline Epistles: Letter of Faith and Encouragement Ephesians Book 10 28

The Amor of Faith 28

Pauline Epistles: Letter of Faith and Encouragement Philippians Book 11 30

The Secret of True Joy!! 30

Pauline Epistles: Letter of Faith and Encouragement Colossians Book 12 32

Christ Above All 32

Pauline Epistles: Letter of Faith and Encouragement 1 Thessalonians Book 13 34

The Trumpet will Sound 34

Pauline Epistles: Letter of Faith and Encouragement 2 Thessalonians Book 14 36

The Day of The Lord 36

Pauline Epistles: Letter of Faith and Encouragement 1 Timothy Book 15 38

Preach, Teach, and Lead! 38

Pauline Epistles: Letter of Faith and Encouragement 2 Timothy Book 16 40

Fight The Good Fight 40

Pauline Epistles: Letter of Faith and Encouragement Titus Book 17 42

Faith in Action 42

Pauline Epistles: Letter of Faith and Encouragement 44

Philemon Book 18 44

Forgiven and Set Free 44

General Epistles of Wisdom and Endurance Hebrews book 19 46

The Author of Our Faith 46

General Epistles: Wisdom & Endurance James Book 20 48

Faith in Action 48

General Epistles: Wisdom & Endurance I Peter Book 21	50
Victory Through Perseverance	50
General Epistles: Wisdom & Endurance II Peter Book 22	52
Hold steadfast to God's Word	52
General Epistles: Wisdom & Endurance I John Book 23	54
God's Divine Love	54
General Epistles: Wisdom & Endurance II John Book 24	56
A Warning Against Deception	56
General Epistles: Wisdom & Endurance III John Book 25	58
Hospitality from the heart	58
General Epistles: Wisdom & Endurance Jude Book 26	59
Contending for the Faith	59
Revelation: The Beginning and the End Revelation Book 27	61
At The Cross	65
Epilogue	67
Closing Invitation	69
My Prayer	70
Bibliography	72

Preface

In the quiet and solitude of a world disrupted by a pandemic, I found myself in a season of reflection, searching for solace and deeper meaning. It was during this time, in the stillness of my heart and mind, that the Holy Spirit led me to a path of study and creativity. As I opened the pages of the Bible, I felt a divine urge to not only understand its teachings but to express them in a form that would resonate with others. This collection of poems is the result of that inspiration—a poetic journey through the essential truths of each book of the Bible.

Each poem has been carefully crafted to capture the essence of the Scriptures, distilling their wisdom, love, and guidance into verses that speak to the heart. My hope is that, through this artistic interpretation of the Word, I might reach those who are seeking, those who thirst for a deeper connection with God. It is my prayer that these words will touch hearts, stir souls, and inspire a renewed faith in the power and grace of the Lord.

In a world where we are often isolated, may these poems serve as a reminder that we are never truly alone. God's Word is alive, and His presence is with us, always. I invite you to journey through these pages with an open heart, ready to be moved and transformed by the Spirit.

May this work bring light, hope, and love into your life as it has into mine.

I do not proclaim to be a theologian, a Bible scholar, or a member of the clergy. I am simply an individual, formed in the image of God, who has been inspired and spiritually moved to share His Word with the world. In this, I am not unlike the disciples of old—humble vessels, empowered by the Holy Spirit to carry the message of love, truth, and salvation. Just as the writers of the Scriptures were guided by divine inspiration, I, too, have felt the stirring of the Spirit, compelling me to write and share the words that flow from a place of deep reverence and faith.

The Lord continues to work miracles today, inspiring and motivating people to step into their God-given purpose and true destiny. We are all called to be living vessels of His Word—whether through acts of kindness, words of encouragement, or creative expressions that bring glory to His name. It is my hope that these poems will serve as a reminder of the ever-present power of the Holy Spirit, working in and through each of us, just as He did in the lives of the disciples.

These poems are the product of academic study and a heart surrendered to God's calling. They are born out of a desire to share the beauty and depth of the Bible in a way that resonates with those who seek to know Him more.

My prayer is that these words will speak to your heart, draw you closer to the Lord, and inspire you to live boldly in the light of His purpose for your life.

May the Spirit of God move within you as you read, and may you be encouraged to step into your own destiny as a vessel of His Word.

The vision for this book was born out of an inherent faith and a deep, compelling desire to learn, grow, and embrace the divine messages that God has lovingly provided as a roadmap for life's journey. These poems are a reflection of my own spiritual walk—a journey of discovery, renewal, and connection with the Word of God.

Through each verse, I have sought to encapsulate the timeless truths and profound wisdom found in Scripture, presenting them in a way that speaks to the heart and ignites the spirit. It is my hope that as you read these poems, you will find yourself immersed in God's love, encouraged by His promises, and inspired to seek Him more fully in your own life.

I believe that within these pages lies the potential for transformation. My prayer is that each poem you read will resonate deeply within you, imparting a spiritual message that renews your spirit, restores your hope, and awakens the zest and zeal God has placed within your soul.

May this collection be a source of light and encouragement, drawing you closer to the Creator and guiding you along your unique journey of faith.

Over the past six years, I have dedicated myself to an in-depth journey of research, analysis, and study, delving into the works of world-renowned biblical theologians, scholars, and clergy. This all-encompassing and comprehensive project proved to be both a profound challenge and a deeply enriching experience. Through cross-referencing their material, I discovered a prevailing thread of truth—a shared focus on the core contexts and themes of each book of the Bible. This unified understanding became the foundation upon which I could build and compose the poetry presented.

Through this remarkable journey, the Holy Spirit has gently guided me to a place of comfort, peace, and purpose. Along the way, I have discovered that the gifts God has placed within me can be called to action in ways far beyond my own expectations. As I delved deeper into biblical exploration, the Lord revealed to me a powerful truth: the secret to my blessings has always been rooted in obedience to His Word, unwavering faithfulness, and a kind heart.

God's favor has been a steady presence in my life, strengthening me daily and inspiring me to fulfill His purpose. By His grace alone, this book is now in your hands. It is a testament to His faithfulness and an offering to those seeking the passion and power of the Word of God.

As you read these pages, I pray that the Spirit speaks to your heart with a rhythm of love and the beath of truth. May these words inspire you, encourage you, and open your eyes to blessings far beyond your imagination. May the seeds of faith blossom within you, transforming your journey and drawing you closer to the One who makes all things possible.

Acknowledgments

In all of our ways, acknowledge Christ, and He shall direct our path- Proverbs 3:5-6

Proverbs 3:5-6 reminds us to acknowledge Christ, and He will direct our paths. I thank God for His grace, guidance, and wisdom, which made this work possible.

To the biblical scholars and clergy whose work inspired me: I have studied and referenced your work; I stand on your shoulders and am deeply indebted to your dedication to preserving and sharing God's word.

My heartfelt thanks go to my husband, Roderick LeBrew, for his unwavering support and encouragement and to my incredible sons, whose curiosity has fueled my passion for God's Word.

I honor my late parents, Malverna and George Merritt, for grounding me in faith and love. Finally, thank you, readers. May these poems inspire your faith and draw you closer to God. May the words in these pages touch your heart as deeply as they have touched mine.

The Gospels: Matthew Book 1

The King Has Come

The gospel of Matthew is his sacred recollection,

Of Jesus' life, death, and resurrection.

Seek, and ye shall find God's kingdom is for all of mankind.

From His birth in Bethlehem to His lineage to Abraham.

From Mary's immaculate conception,

To freeing the Jews from oppression.

From healing the sick to comforting the poor,

To resolving conflict, He's a proven Savior.

And the miracles He performed were said,

To be supernatural, then His teachings were spread.

So, how can some Hebrews be misled,

Into thinking Jesus is somehow dead?

Many of life's views, we may not share,

But let us find solace in His teachings of the Lord's prayer!

Everyone can proclaim:

Our Father, who art in heaven, hallowed be thy name!

For His goodness and mercy, we mustn't discount.

Instead, we should embrace His sermons upon the mount.

He said, *"Pick up your cross and follow me,*

For my yoke is easy!"

So do not fear,

The kingdom of heaven is near.

Yes, the promised Savior is here at last,

Just as Isaiah, Daniel & Ezekiel had forecast.

Jesus speaks of His death & resurrection,

Because of His love & affection.

His Grace & Protection for *our* transgression.

Jesus made the sacrifice,

So that we may have everlasting life.

And as He suffered and died upon the cross.

He shed His blood and paid the costs.

Then a darkness covered the earth,

And Made It So Cold.

It just *couldn't contain our Savior's soul!*

The tomb broke open, the sun stood still,

The mountains were sloping, and it seemed so unreal!

Now, even some Jews can testify,

Jesus ROSE, upon the sky..... *Let Him be glorified!*

Amen!

The Gospels: Mark Book 2

The Passion of Christ

The Messiah has come for all to see,

His work, life, and ministry.

When He was baptized: It signified.

The Holy Spirit would descend.

Giving almighty power to devour

Any weapon formed against men!

He displayed authority.

By feeding the hungry, calming the storm,

and walking upon the sea.

He shows compassion and service to all,

Then commissioned His disciple to follow *the same protocol.*

He promised redemption to those that repent,

and accept His *new covenant.*

This book is devoted to Jesus' actions,

Vivid details of the passion.

And although some people didn't believe,

They simply couldn't conceive,

That the Messiah had come for all to see,

In full greatness and authority.

As the scriptures would be fulfilled,

When *Jesus says that He would be killed.*

Spit upon, mocked, and body torn,

Beat upon the head as they crowned it with thorns.

The blood, oh the blood of the Son of God

"Poured out" as they pierced Him in the side.

The soldiers brutally attacked,

As Jesus carried the sins of the world on His back.

When there was no more life to give,

He died so that we could live.

But soon after that fateful day,

The tombstone had rolled away.

His body was nowhere to be found,

HE GOT UP from that burial ground!

People were in disbelief!

But He showed the *nail prints* on His hands and feet.

You see, His ascension proved victory over death and grief.

Then, He walked from nation to nation.

Preaching the gift of salvation.

And with open arms, **HE FORGIVES**.

We serve a Savior that lives...

HE LIVES!
HE LIVES!

The Gospels:
Luke: Book 3

The Compassionate Savior

Luke provides a scared narrative,

About the ministry of Christ and how He lived.

Jesus' compassion for the Gentiles,

And people seen as not worthwhile.

The Lord is the Son of *all humanity*,

Who has come to save the lost by way of Christianity.

He speaks of Himself as Messiah,

His death and resurrection.

Yet, His ministry was met with some rejection,

Alleged to be an insurrection.

So, Jesus faced trials and tribulations,

But was found *innocent of any violations!!*

With this verdict, the Pharisees were mortified,

And demanded that Jesus be *crucified!*

And, although His death was unjustified,

This fateful event would satisfy...

The deliverance of sin,

As a *free gift* to be born again!

So that the Holy Spirit could descend,

Upon our hearts as we transcend.

Giving us power, purpose, and peace,

Pouring upon our lives an abundance of increase.

So, with Holy Communion, we commemorate,

The Savior has RISEN and *celebrate*

The blood that was shed and *grants us Grace,*

To one day see Him, *Face to Face!*

Amen!

The Gospels: John Book 4

The Light of The World

The voice crying out in the wilderness,

Is the testimony of John the Baptist.

Behold! The lamb of God has come to save the world of sin (John 1:29)

Whosoever believeth in Him shall not perish but live again.

I saw the Holy Spirit descend upon Jesus like a dove,

"This is my beloved Son," uttered the voice of truth from above.

He is the suffering servant who has come to set us free,

The Messiah foretold in the book of Isaiah- chapter 53.

So, John became an early disciple of Jesus' ministry,

As he witnessed the miracles and signs of Christ's divinity.

Jesus performed miracles to show spiritual transformation,

Thus, displaying the immortality, that takes place in salvation.

Like raising Lazarus from the dead.

Yet some rejected these signs of deity,

And fell into darkness instead.

Declaring Jesus a heresy

And accusing Him of blasphemy!

Although Jesus had done nothing wrong,

Since *He existed … all along!*

He came in the flesh with truth and grace,

To sacrifice His blood and redeem the human race.

Jesus is the mediator between God and man,

Some find this notion beyond human comprehension.

But upon the cross, as His blood was shed,

They witnessed His eternal life when He *ROSE from the dead!*

And, although He has ascended to the *right hand of the Father,*

Remember, His last commandment is to *love one another.*

Now, He leaves the Holy Spirit in our hearts as a guide,

Restoring *faithfulness, truth, and love,*

Then believers stand sanctified.

The Book of John records miracles and signs of Jesus' deity.

It shows a path to God's kingdom through *His love, grace, and mercy!!!*

Amen!

History of the early church: Acts Book 5

Acts of the Apostles- Anointed with Power!

The Book of Acts narrates,

The actions of the apostles as they advocate,

The principles of the church that Christ creates.

Jesus promised to empower the apostles,

Then bestowed the Holy Spirit during the Pentecostal.

This sacred event was prophesized by Joel many years ago,

When he said:

The *Lord will pour out His spirit* from head to toe.

Then all of humanity will know…

That Christians are empowered, guided, and directed by Christ,

The Messiah who paid the ultimate sacrifice.

The *suffering servant* mentioned in Isaiah's predictions,

The Lord that touches our hearts and guides our convictions.

Like Paul, the prominent Pharisee,

Inspired by Christ, then he *converted* to Christianity.

The Lord's salvation is granted to *all* that believe and repent,

then accept His *new covenant!*

Established through *the blood of Christ* for the redemption of sin,

We *never* have to sacrifice another animal again!

For *God's law is now engraved on the hearts of men,*

as declared by Jeremiah in the Old Testament.

Now, Paul had a major role in Christian ministry.

Despite opposition, he preached religiously!

He wrote letters setting the foundation of the church,

Emphasizing the power of prayer as it expands through the Lord's approach.

The book of Acts affirms ministry through the holy spirit.

It also speaks of spreading the gospel to *anyone* willing to hear it.

Amen!

General Epistles: Wisdom & Endurance
Romans Book 6

By Faith, not by Works!

For all have sinned and fallen short of the glory of God, (Roman3;23-24)

But by faith, we stand justified.

Within the heart, we believe, and with the tongue, we confess:

That Jesus is Lord, to declare our faithfulness!

Here, the Apostle Paul wrote letters, setting forth his spiritual conviction-

Proclaiming righteousness is revealed by faith.

And **atonement, solely through the crucifixion**!

As we embrace the **new covenant,**

By way of **Jesus' blood sacrifice,**

We devote our lives to service unto Christ.

Displaying faith by obedience to His Word,

The fruit one bears, the blessings conferred.

He writes about God's love, mercy, and grace

Are conveyed when His Son died in our place.

So that our sins are erased

And our hearts can embrace:

The transformation...

That takes place in salvation!

Which is *a free gift* and opportunity,

For **all believers to join in unity**...

To press on and **walk in the newness of life**,

As Paul's letters expressed with fervent delight.

Pleading for all **to come to the light!**

Restoring a relationship with *God*... ***that is right!***

Pauline Epistles: Letter of Faith and Encouragement
1st Corinthians Book 7

Living as The Body of Christ

The Apostle Paul encouraged faith, love, and unity

As themes of his letters to the church community.

Preachers were divided on how to worship and serve the Lord.

But Paul proposed that the spirit of God flows on one accord.

With a spirit of unity, we can discover

And seek out the opportunity to embrace one another.

As believers, we are called to display

A standard of integrity that represents God's loving way.

Christ has bestowed spiritual gifts for us to make use of

But before all else, we must cling to His love.

We are **one body, one spirit, one temple** by design

In all that we do and say, **let God's glory shine!**

Stand firm in faith. **Be courageous! Be strong!**

As God requires obedience, it is wickedness that is wrong.

The church of Corinth was crying out for direction,

When Paul heard of the problems that needed correction.

He centered on the power of God's protection,

And promise of eternal life through the resurrection.

His letters were not meant to reprimand,

But to deliver revelation of God's command.

To consider **our calling, our purpose, our conviction,**

Examine our way of life as we journey along this mission.

Love is the truth that binds,

Resolves conflict and creates like minds.

Here, Paul responds to the many **concerns**

To **get the church in order before The Master returns!**

Pauline Epistles: Letter of Faith and Encouragement
2nd Corinthians Book 8

From Trials to Triumph

Although the Apostle Paul suffered many afflictions,

He remained steadfast in his holy convictions.

Pleading to the Lord to set him free

From his pain, suffering, and agony

Of a thorn in his flesh, a disability.

Yet, he pressed on with faithful humility.

Since Paul was chosen, his ministry was proficient,

God said, **"*His grace is sufficient*!" 2 cor 12:9**

The Lord provides comfort in the midst of our pain,

Just love, trust, and believe Him and His blessings we'll gain.

Paul gave of himself unconditionally,

And invited believers to make contributions willingly.

Give from the heart to reap what we sow.

Only faithful Christians will know...

His promises, provision, and favor in our lives overflow,

When we **honor our stewardship... To give and let go!**

After writing these letters to the church community,

Paul received good news on their unity.

Then, many false prophets could not succeed,

Because the church members of Corinth had agreed

To reconcile and follow God's holy creed.

Thus, eternal life is guaranteed!!

When Paul faced doubts about his apostolic authority,

He conquered notions of his inferiority.

By boldly announcing a confession,

About being *caught up* in God's third heaven.

Chosen by Christ to lead in ministry

With love, forgiveness, and unity!!
Amen!

Pauline Epistles: Letter of Faith and Encouragement
Galatians Book 9

Set Free in Christ Jesus!

The Apostle Paul delivered God's message.

And it applies to all.

We are redeemed and justified by faith.

Not through Moses' law.

Those who have faith are children of Abraham.

Thus, **"All nations will be blessed,"** (gen 22:18) said The Great... **I AM**.

Paul's letters to the churches of Galatians,

Were designed to correct misinterpretations,

About requirements to be circumcised,

Because this does not matter in the Lord's eyes.

There is no need to follow customs of a Jewish nation.

Since God's **redemption comes *solely* through salvation**.

We are *saved by His grace* through the blood sacrifice.

No human works can redeem us, only faith in Jesus Christ.

The Holy Spirit bears fruit in the life of believers.

Otherwise, it exposes fakes and deceivers.

You see, *the righteous shall walk by faith and not by sight.*

For His glory shines upon our path, guiding us to the light.

Assuring us... we'll be alright!

Until the day He comes... to reunite!!

Pauline Epistles: Letter of Faith and Encouragement
Ephesians Book 10

The Amor of Faith

In the Garden of Eden, humanity was united with the divine.

Until an evil force of darkness took over their rebellious minds.

This act of defiance separated them from the divine,

Crossing over into the darkness of which this world is now enshrined.

The book of Ephesians provides insight,

Into **God's purpose to reunite**.

With a predestined plan to invite,

All ethnicities to the light!

Through the blood of Jesus Christ,

Who paid the ultimate sacrifice.

And by God's mercy and His grace,

He has redeemed this human race!

Believers are sealed with the Holy Spirit as God's promise and guarantee,

Of our inheritance into the kingdom, as we have been set free!

Free... from every iniquity!

To live in heaven throughout eternity.

The church is called to keep the unity,

Doing all things through Christ who strengthens thee.

And walking in a manner of integrity.

The body of Christ and designated pathway,

The church as His living vessel in full display.

It's devoted to the Godly head,

Standing firm and not mislead.

Fighting against the prince of darkness who divides,

Putting on the armor of Christ,

One Faith... One Spirit... One God!!

Amen!

Pauline Epistles: Letter of Faith and Encouragement
Philippians Book 11

The Secret of True Joy!!

Through hardship, suffering, opposition, and pain

In a jailhouse, tormented and bound by those chains.

Paul tells of rejoicing amid trials and tribulations.

As he's chosen to spread the gospel, hence the word of salvation.

In this letter from prison, Paul wishes to testify,

So, he wrote to the church of Phillipi.

Saying that despite *persecution and torment,*

He **rejoices in the Lord as a devoted servant.**

Paul was rich, and now *all had been lost,*

But for Jesus, it's worth it when we *"***Count the cost***!"*

Because as disciples and Christians, **we carry the cross!**

Proclaiming our sins have been paid off.

So, no matter our stature, our lot, or standard of living

We're called to minister, rejoice, and praise God with thanksgiving!

Paul teaches us to unite in humility,

Casting all cares and hostility.

For our belief drives our behavior.

Let us sacrifice and mimic our savior!

Be courageous! Be fearless! Be bold!

Stand for his namesake, as this sparks **"joy" in our souls!**

Paul **expresses appreciation** to *all*.

Who backed **his ministry** as he answers God's *call!!*

Through Paul's prison ministry, we see..

"*I can do all things through Christ, who strengthens me!*"

So, no matter if we're rich or poor, free or in prison,

God *will* supply his almighty provision!

Pauline Epistles: Letter of Faith and Encouragement Colossians Book 12

Christ Above All

Jesus is divine, human, and utter perfection,

Disarming the power of evil through His death and resurrection.

Paul wrote this letter to warn of false teaching,

The mixing of theology during erroneous preaching.

Instructing us to clothe ourselves with compassion,

kindness, and humility,

Then, embrace the fullness of His divinity.

Forsake religious rules, rituals, and lamb's sacrifice.

As the blood of Jesus paid the price,

For the penalty of sin

So, believers will not die but live again!

Christians should shed worldly impurity,

And seek to grow in spiritual maturity.

Cling to love as the perfect bond of unity,

A living vessel of His church and community.

Set our minds on things above, keep our eyes on the goal.

Care for family with heavenly love. Trust in Him to guard the soul.

So, when faced with false teachings and misinterpretation,

Trust He is the creator, sustainer, and author of salvation!

Pauline Epistles: Letter of Faith and Encouragement
1 Thessalonians Book 13

The Trumpet will Sound

Persecution by authorities was discouraging.

Yet, the Christian church of Thessalonica was flourishing.

They were steadfast in their commitment to follow Christ,

But had questions regarding their afterlife.

So, this book assures us in every chapter,

Believers will be caught up in the rapture!!

The *Lord will ascend from heaven with a loud command,*

Then, the voice of an angel will consume this land.

With a divine call from God above,

Awakening our spirits like a morning dove.

This is the second coming of Jesus, whereby,

All Christians return to the Lord in the sky!

We ought to please God by walking in the light.

"*For the Savior returns like a thief in the night.*" 1Thes 5:2

Practice faith, hope, and love in the face of affliction.

Just as Jesus bore pain during the crucifixion.

The mark of a Christian!

The heart of conviction!

Destined to be delivered from sin,

When Jesus, our *Savior, returns again!!*

Pauline Epistles: Letter of Faith and Encouragement
2 Thessalonians Book 14

The Day of The Lord

Let us not be deceived by false teachers, rumors, and conspirers.

For the Lord will return like a blazing fire!

Glowing with grace, so heavenly divine,

Beaming from Mt. Olive, where His glory shall shine!

Peace and Love will surely abound,

But the wicked and evil will be brought down.

Where every knee shall bow, and tongue confess,

That Jesus is Lord and holiness.

So, stand firm in the Lord's return and honor His ways,

Be grateful and hopeful when giving Him praise!

This book gives clarity about the day of the Lord,

Which will be preceded by rebellion and blatant discord.

So let not our hearts be weary nor souls shaken.

"On the day of the Lord, the dead in Christ will awaken!"1Thes4:16

Our souls taken!

Our sins forsaken!

No more persecution or spiritual strife.

When we unite with our Savior for *everlasting life*!!

Hallelujah!

Pauline Epistles: Letter of Faith and Encouragement
1 Timothy Book 15

Preach, Teach, and Lead!

It matters what we say and do,

As Pastoral leadership starts with you.

Promote sound doctrine every day,

Confront those deceivers who've lost their way.

Pray for the lowly and even high leaders,

Teach the gospel to non-believers.

Set an example of how to act,

Silence those who've come to distract.

Be sure to support and uplift,

The saints of God to use their gifts.

Meet qualifications to Pastor and lead.

Fight the good fight and honor God's creed.

Timothy received this letter from the Apostle Paul,

On bringing order to the church, as he answers God's call.

Pauline Epistles: Letter of Faith and Encouragement
2 Timothy Book 16

Fight The Good Fight

The Apostle Paul devoted his life to spreading the Word,

And fought for sound doctrine undeterred.

He taught preachers and even apostles,

Sharing his revelation of the gospel.

He testified before emperors and kings.

Through diligence and suffering, he earned his wings.

His work was done!

His course had been run!

He fought the good fight and kept the faith.

Now, a crown in heaven for him awaits.

By God's grace, Paul is finishing the race. (2Tim 4:7)

So, he writes to Timothy to take his place.

Stand firm! Dear Timothy,

As you preach God's ministry.

Know that the spirit of the Lord gives power,

Even in our darkest hour.

Thus, your friends can't make or break you.

Because the Lord will never forsake you.

Some may not want to hear the truth,

But His death and resurrection were living proof.

So be armed and be ready to persevere,

Like a good soldier, *Have No Fear!!*

Many are called to minister, but Timothy was chosen.

Because of his *faith, love, and godly devotion!!*

Pauline Epistles: Letter of Faith and Encouragement
Titus Book 17

Faith in Action

The gospel inspires godliness in the lives of believers,

Otherwise, it exposes fakes and deceivers.

Belief in the Savior

Can be seen through behavior.

So, putting forth guidance for church officials,

Was the focus of this epistle.

Instructing Titus on how to lead,

And appoint elders to preserve God's creed.

To set an example through good deeds.

To help those saints that stand in need.

In accordance with the will of God

Challenging those who put on a façade.

Stand for what you *teach*!

Practice what you *preach*!

Embrace the Word and be blessed.

As sound preaching leads to godliness

Titus was called to the island of Crete,

To correct false teaching and confront deceit.

Focusing on the redemptive power of God's grace

While spreading the gospel from place to place.

Commissioned to do good as his heart desired.

Even as King of the Roman Empire!

Pauline Epistles: Letter of Faith and Encouragement

Philemon Book 18

Forgiven and Set Free…

To err is human, but to forgive is divine.

Our steps are ordered by God's design.

Pleading for acceptance of a servant on the run

Is the anchor of this note to Philemon.

Paul appeals to Philemon to forgive a brother in Christ.

Should he owe you, I'll pay the price.

Paul's offer may have been a parable of sacrifice.

Just as Jesus paid the cost to paradise.

The living word in full display.

The early church leading the way.

Here, the wrongdoer was delivered into a new humanity.

Through the redemptive blood of Jesus, by way of Christianity.

For he is walking by faith and not by sight.

Elevated above the storm and now sees the light.

Paul writes as an abolitionist to stamp out inequality.

Sharing the gospel of Jesus as a liberating ideology.

Philemon looked upon Paul with much adulation,

Since he witnessed God's grace and transformation,

reconciliation, and the hope of salvation!

In the book of Philemon, love has won,

As *forgiveness and equality* are for everyone!!

General Epistles of Wisdom and Endurance
Hebrews book 19

The Author of Our Faith

The book of Hebrews provides encouragement to praise and persevere.

By embracing faith, hope, and love as the Savior draws us near.

Reminding us that Old Testament prophecy had come to pass,

Through a Prince of Peace, a Perfect Priest,

of whom nothing could surpass.

Not even glorious Angels on high.

Nor the great Moses could qualify.

As a once and for all sacrifice.

Whereby the power of His blood paid the price,

His promise and guarantee for everlasting life!!

Rejoicing with praise in paradise.

No longer a need to confess to a rabbi or priest,

Nor sacrifice a precious beast.

Now, His divine glory beams upon our path.

Redeeming us from sin and wrath.

Ooooh, He hears our prayers and makes provisions,

Instills the Holy Spirit to sway our convictions.

Strengthen our condition.

And guide our mission.

To the one and only "*Majesty on High.*"

Whereby our *purpose, devotion, and hopes lie.*

General Epistles: Wisdom & Endurance
James Book 20

Faith in Action

Faith and deeds flow on the same accord.

Proclaims James, the brother of Christ- the Lord.

So, this book instructs us, with several commands,

On how to follow God's demands.

To be caring towards everyone else,

By *loving your neighbor as you love yourself.*

Then faithful deeds will surely flow,

From the hearts of believers who claim to know.

That our behavior is based on our faith,

And hypocrisy is a sinful disgrace.

Heavenly wisdom, kind words, and lawful adherence,

May be a test, like that of Job, who proved perseverance.

So, in every believer's experience

We should possess these traits in our appearance.

By having faithful endurance in the midst of trials

Expressing obedience in one's lifestyle,

Calling forth a tongue of praise,

Putting off a voice of rage.

Not just talking the Christian talk,

But as believers, we're walking the Christian walk.

Humbled and devoted, with praying heads bowed,

Understanding that God opposes being proud.

For wealth and riches will all pass away,

And our faithful works will be judged one day.

So, in every trial and every test,

Let faith by our actions manifest!!

General Epistles: Wisdom & Endurance
I Peter Book 21

Victory Through Perseverance

Peter, 'the rock' upon which Jesus could build,

Stood firm in the midst of suffering until God's glory was revealed.

As His chosen people, we're called to persevere,

Having hope through the resurrection that His kingdom is near.

So, we try to resist the devil, who seeks to devour,

By destroying our faith, thus taking our power.

And, at the time this letter was written,

Believing in Christ was strictly forbidden.

But God opposes pride and gives grace to the humble.

He carries us through the times that we stumble.

So, when we're honorable and submit to His will,

Our hopes, dreams, and prayers, He tends to fulfill.

We grow spiritually through obedience by doing what is right.

Using our anointed gifts and walking in His light.

Here, Peter reminds us that through suffering, be assured.

Just like Jesus suffered and died, then *His glory was restored.*

As believers, we shall reap eternal rewards.

When we unite with our Savior forevermore!!

General Epistles: Wisdom & Endurance
II Peter Book 22

Hold steadfast to God's Word

The heavens will vanish like a roar.

The earth will burn to its' core.

But God promised to restore.

Our hearts and souls forevermore!

Peter witnessed the exalted majesty on a mount,

A blessed, spiritual, sacred account.

Then he proclaimed *the day of the Lord is near*,

With thrusting judgment like a celestial sphere.

So be vigilant against false teachings,

The spreading of lies and fake preaching!

Peter urges us to live a life that embodies the good news,

By growing in faith, knowledge, and Christian virtues.

Eagerly watch and wait for the return of Christ,

Who may appear to us like a thief in the night!

So be steadfast in our faith and resolute,

Partakers of a divine nature that bears fruit.

Because following sinful, corrupted worldly desire,

Will be met with *everlasting, consuming fire!*

But God's grace and promise to all who obey,

Is that our *hearts and souls shall never pass away!!*

General Epistles: Wisdom & Endurance
I John Book 23

God's Divine Love

Through faith, we've been set free,

And promised a life of eternity.

By embracing a loving spirit that is pleasing in His sight,

Living a life that's devoted to what is right. By walking in His light.

Here, John reminds us to beware of false teaching,

Those that profit from fake preaching.

Because nobody stands without sin,

It is by God's grace that we've been forgiven.

And through God's love, He sacrificed His Son,

So that sin can be undone,

And believers judged as Holy ones.

The Apostle John testified to Jesus's existence,

As he wept at the cross during the crucifixion!

So, let us worship and praise with thanksgiving because of

This sacrifice and display of God's divine LOVE!!!

General Epistles: Wisdom & Endurance
II John Book 24

A Warning Against Deception

Dear beloved woman of God,

Beware of those who put on a façade.

The preachers, who appear to be nice

But refuse to acknowledge the coming of Christ.

Here, John reminds us that Christ came in the flesh.

Those who teach otherwise:

Refuse to attest!

Refuse to confess!

Seeking to oppress!

So, *be vigilant and walk in the truth of His Word.*

With love and obedience undeterred.

Fellowship with virtue while praising the Lord.

Pray in unity on one accord.

To the beloved, the ladies, the *chosen ones*

Granted to birth our *Savior*, the only begotten *Son*!!

Amen!

General Epistles: Wisdom & Endurance
III John Book 25

Hospitality from the heart

The shortest book of the Bible, yet it shouts with clarity.

Always walk in the truth with humble sincerity.

Reject church leaders who are boastful, proud, or critical.

But greater joy to those who preach that which is biblical.

As God rebukes the egotistical, controlling, and visceral.

So, let us cling to His love, which is unconditional.

And fellowship with a spirit of congeniality.

Praising in unity and hospitality.

God calls for us to stay focused on Him.

Our *walk*, our *purpose*, our *beginning*, our *end!!*

General Epistles: Wisdom & Endurance
Jude Book 26

Contending for the Faith

Beware! Beware! Beware!

Of false preachers who come to disrupt.

Convincing others to not care!

About a sinful nature that corrupts.

Teaching that God's redemptive grace may come as a license to sin.

Here, Jude *declares our conduct reflects our faith and sincere religion.*

Christians who are born again

Are transformed and contend,

That our belief is found through our behavior

Let us display love by mimicking our Savior.

God rebukes those who rebel,

For in the realm of darkness, their souls may dwell.

Hold fast to the Word, or believing shall be in vain,

Because it speaks through the church,

Where our Savior reigns.

He reigns!

He reigns!

Revelation: The Beginning and the End
Revelation Book 27

Prophecy and Promise

The spirit of the Lord revealed this revelation

For the end of times to be ushered in by tribulation.

Through a vision of heaven, a glimpse of His throne.

A scroll to be broken by the lamb of God alone.

The Book of Life, its pages turn,

Each soul is judged, the fate is learned.

Where the wicked will be slain by the brightness of God.

There'll be no darkness, no place to hide.

When Satan will be unleashed,

Carrying the number of the beast.

Upon the foreheads of followers will be affixed,

The cursed number 666.

But Satan will be bound and thrown at sea.

Where evilness spends an eternity.

When the seal is broken and the trumpet sounds,

God's grace and mercy will abound.

Remember those early teachers of salvation?

Their Martyred souls will cry out for vindication.

Those devoted prophets who were under attack,

Well, this time, **death cannot hold them back**!!!

As Christ promised to return as Messianic King.

So have faith and hope when worshipping!

That the battle of good over evil is won.

So, it is written, and so it shall be done!!!

Blessed are those who hold it dear!

The revelation, the hope, the fear!

That believers will rise, a new world restored!

God's eternal peace **_forevermore_**!!!

So let all the saints who are **_born again..._**

Say, **_blessed is the Word of God_**. **AMEN!**

Amen! Amen! Amen!

During my studies, on May 22, 2022, an overwhelmingly compelling poem came to my heart. I'd like to share it with you for inspiration and devotion.

At The Cross

They shouted out 'blasphemy."

Although Christ delivered them from slavery.

And at the cross on Mt. Calvary,

Jesus overcame the harsh brutality

From those of a certain nationality,

That refuse to embrace his principality

Over all that exists,

As foretold in the book of genesis!!

And although the whips and lashes were harshly felt

The power of His blood had to be dealt.

For the redemption of sin,

As *a free gift* to be born again.

He hung His head and died,

So that we may stand justified.

They wrapped His body in linen from head to toe,

Then the oceans poured out and left a rainbow

That cast a shadow

Until the spirit of the Lord was let go!

When He ascended from that tomb,

The heart of creation was in full bloom!!

The light of the world that set us free,

Because of His love, grace, and mercy!

Hallelujah!!

Epilogue

The Bible tells the ultimate truth of love, redemption, and everlasting life through Jesus Christ. From creation to the promise of eternal salvation, it unveils God's unyielding love for humanity—a love that endured even through our rebellion, sin, and suffering. It is the story of a Creator who became the Savior, offering Himself so that we might be reconciled to Him and live forever in His presence.

The disciples who walked with Jesus bore witness to His life, His miracles, His sacrificial death, and His glorious resurrection. They did not just see—they believed. Empowered by the Holy Spirit, they went forth into the world to proclaim the good news of salvation, teaching that eternal life is found in Jesus Christ alone. Their words and deeds, preserved in the Scriptures, remain a testament to their unwavering faith and the transformative power of God's grace.

The Bible is not merely an account of the past; it is a living guide for the present and a hope for the future. It invites us into a relationship with the God who calls us His children. Its truths resonate across time, reminding us that we are never beyond the reach of God's mercy and love.

As the final pages of Scripture close with the promise of Jesus' return, we are left with a call to faith and action: to love as He loved, to live as He lived, and to carry His message of hope to the ends of the earth.

The story of the Bible continues in us. As Christians, we carry the cross and await the day when every sin will be wiped away and all things will be made new. Until then, let us stand firm in the promises of God, holding fast to His Word and sharing His love with a world still longing for redemption.

This is not the end, for in Christ, it is only the beginning.

Closing Invitation

John 3:16 beautifully proclaims, *"For God so loved the world that He gave His only begotten Son, that whoever believes in Him should not perish but have everlasting life."* This is a profound declaration of God's infinite love and His desire for all of us to know Him personally and eternally.

May I invite you today to open your heart to God's Word and to embrace the gift of salvation through Jesus Christ? Faith is not meant to be a solitary journey. It is in community, fellowship, and worship that we grow closer to God and to one another.

If you are seeking a place to worship, praise, and experience the love of Christ, among others, I warmly encourage you to visit **Agape Baptist Church**, located at **1601 Wadsworth Avenue, Philadelphia, PA 19150**. There, you will find a family of believers who will support and encourage you in your spiritual walk.

Come as you are, and may your journey be one filled with grace, love, and the peace that only God can provide.

My Prayer

Lord,

In this prayer, one word comes to mind, and that word is: **Love!!!**
For **God is Love**—pure, perfect, eternal.
You have shown us what Love truly is by giving Your only Son,
a sacrifice that echoes through eternity, setting us free from condemnation.
You loved us first, and in that truth, our hearts overflow with love in return.

Thank You for the joy of spiritual connection with You.
What a blessing it is to serve a God
who not only meets our needs,
but also delights in fulfilling the desires of our hearts.

You have promised in Your Word:
"Blessed are they who hunger and thirst after righteousness: for they shall be filled." (Matthew 5:6)
And in that filling, we find peace—
a deep, abiding peace that surpasses all understanding.

I pray that in this world, longing for light,
faith and hope would rise like the morning sun.
That hearts would receive, and eyes behold,
the wonders of Your glory—and seek redemption and Love.

Thank You, God, for the gift of family.
For *the pure in heart shall see God first* and I believe that

our children
are a piece of heaven placed right here on earth—
living, breathing glimpses of Your glory,
reflections of Your goodness,
and reminders of Your love.

And for those loved ones You've placed beside us
to walk this life with—
they are a manifestation of Your majesty,
an assurance of Your provision,
Your comfort, and protection
as we journey along this path that ultimately leads to Your Kingdom.

Lord, may Your light shine upon our faces,
so that all who see us may see the **Love of God**—
and know that **You still live**.

Let Your glory rest on us like the morning dew, renewing our spirits, transforming our lives, and giving us the zest and zeal to press on and
and never dry up—but rise up to always express the Love that first found us.

In Jesus' precious name,
Amen.

Bibliography

Sources & References for reading and translations:

The Holy Bible- King James Version

Beginners Guide to the Bible- Jeffrey Kranz

Insight.org- Chuck Swindoll

Unger's Bible Handbook, Merrill F. Unger

An Introduction to the Old Testament- Tremper Longman III & Raymond Dillard

How to Get Into the Bible, Stephen M. Miller

Life Application Study Bible, NIV, Tyndale Publishing

NIV Study Bible, Zondervan Publishing

Blue Letter Bible.org

Knowing-Jesus.com

Bible Study Tools- The Salem Web Network

Teachsundayschool.com

Cliff Notes- 2020 Houghton Mifflin Harcourt

Bible Gateway.com

Learning Religion- Dot Dash Publishing Co.

Sage Research Journals

Christianity.com- Jessica Brodie

Bible Hub.com

Top Verses- The Bible Sorted

Sparknotes.com

BelieffNet

Wikipedia

Wikia.org

Bible History.com

Biblelineministries.org

www.ingramcontent.com/pod-product-compliance
Lightning Source LLC
LaVergne TN
LVHW052001060526
838201LV00059B/3781